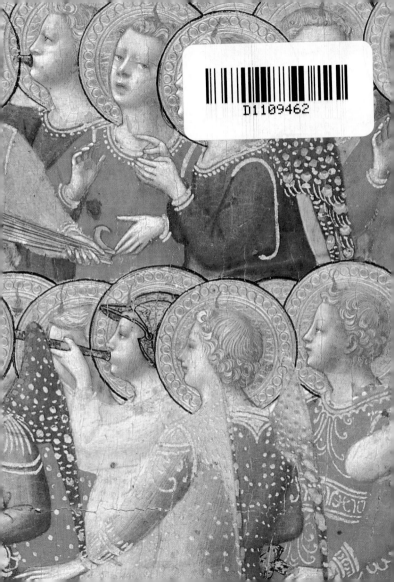

MEDITATIONS
—ON—
LOVE

SISTER
WENDY BECKETT

DK

DORLING KINDERSLEY
LONDON • NEW YORK • STUTTGART

A DORLING KINDERSLEY BOOK

For Tricia, Sean, and Grace.

Editor *Patricia Wright*
Art editor *Claire Legemah*
Managing editor *Sean Moore*
Picture researcher *Jo Walton*
Production controller *Alison Jones*

First American Edition, 1995
2 4 6 8 10 9 7 5 3

Published in the United States by
Dorling Kindersley Publishing, Inc.
95 Madison Avenue, New York,
New York 10016

Published in Great Britain by
Dorling Kindersley Limited.

Library of Congress CIP Data
Beckett, Wendy.
Meditations on love / by Wendy Beckett.
1st American ed.   p. cm.
ISBN 0-7894-0178-9
1. Love--Religious aspects--Meditations.
2. Painting--Appreciation. I. Title.
BL626.4.B43   1995
177'.7--dc20   95-11885 CIP

Color reproduction by GRB Edtirice s.r.l.
Printed and bound in Hong Kong by Imago.

CONTENT

BODILY EMBRACE

IT IS NOT EASY to say exactly what love is. *The Kiss* might seem a perfect illustration: the passionate emotional and physical involvement of two people. In the intensity of their embrace, Klimt's couple have become one, fused together by their mutual ardor. Is this love? Or is it only the appearance of love? Are they giving to each other, or using each other? Are they concerned with the body as integral to the self, or just the body as an instrument? When they part, the two robed forms withdrawing once again into separateness, will each feel greater reverence for the personality of the other or not? A bodily embrace is very precious, but its real value depends upon what it signifies.

The Kiss, 1907-8, Gustav Klimt
71 x 71 in (180 x 180 cm), oil on canvas
Österreichische Galerie, Vienna

TENDER REVERENCE

REVERENCE IS THE deepest form of respect. a serious desire to recognize another as important in his or her own right. It accepts that we as individuals are not central to the universe. It is this attitude of tender humility that Rembrandt expresses with such power in *The Jewish Bride*. His couple are not in their first youth, or beautiful in any classic sense, but both are infinitely moving in their expression. We know at once that they love each other. Each gives love and receives it. Love is supremely beautiful, but like the golden chain the man has placed around the neck of his beloved, it also binds. Each is surrendering freedom, but willingly so, thus facing the truth that we cannot have everything; if we love, we make a choice. They do not even need to look into each other's eyes. Rather, they ponder with wonder, the implications of their blessedness and the meaning of total commitment.

The Jewish Bride (detail), 1665-7, Rembrandt Van Rijn
65 1/2 x 48 in (166.5 x 121.5 cm), oil on canvas
Rijksmuseum, Amsterdam

CHOOSING LOVE

LIKING COMES EASILY: it is spontaneous. Real love, that which will last and make an essential personal difference, is always difficult. It is a matter of choice, either at the beginning or later. At some stage, we have to face up to the seriousness of love. Lárusdóttir's couple are stumpy and unappealing average humanity. He is not merely offering flowers: her hesitation and the presence of the grandfather clock, with its insistence on time, emphasizes that it is himself that he is offering. The wistful onlookers drive the message home: they are those who escape the wonder and the pain of love. The woman looks inward: will she embark upon this relationship, the most absolute of which a human being is capable? He thrusts life toward her, an almost threatening presence. The choice is still open: he has cast his lot, she has not.

Karólína Lárusdóttir, 1993, Man Gives Woman Flowers
14 x 18¹/₂ in (35 x 45 cm), oil on canvas
Private collection

LIFELONG FIDELITY

THE ARNOLFINI WEDDING PORTRAIT is full of symbols of marriage: from the dog, emblem of fidelity, to the fruit and the bed, symbols of fertilty (though history records no children in this marriage). But at its center is the solemn moment in which the young man pauses before placing his hand over that of his girl bride, accepting her as his wife. The discarded shoes and lit candle tell us this is a holy ceremony: each is tremulously aware of the other, devoutly intent on the seriousness of their action. They are making an absolute decision, a mutual undertaking. They know what they are doing: accepting the gift of a lifelong companionship, offering as much as they receive.

The Arnolfini Marriage, 1434, Jan van Eyck
32¼ x 23½ in (82 x 60 cm), oil on wood panel
National Gallery, London

MOTHER LOVE

LOVE IS BOTH INFINITELY REWARDING and endlessly demanding. The two aspects are inseparable. The mother in Berthe Morisot's picture is her sister Edma, rapt in thought as she gazes at her baby daughter. In having a child, parents undertake an unbreakable relationship. As Morisot shows it, the mother's part in this relationship is all gift. She can receive nothing as yet from the child, who is too young to respond. The mother has the duty to protect and cherish, and the alacrity with which it is carried out does not disguise that it is a burden. Edma is not free; her time now belongs to her child. But it is a burden of love, and this mother seems to feel only contentment in her servitude.

The Cradle (cropped), 1872, Berthe Morisot
22 x 18 in (56 x 46 cm), oil on canvas
Musée d'Orsay, Paris

THE LESSON

THE TREE EXUBERATES in blossom, the cabbages are thick on the ground. Van Gogh's young parents concentrate on the work of love: teaching their child to walk. Love is essentially active, intent upon the needs of the other, and the rough intensity of Van Gogh's clumsy forms expresses the dedication of the parents. Spade and wheelbarrow stand idle and forgotten; both parents are conscious of nothing but the needs of their child. The fruitfulness of the setting is highly appropriate: the child is the fruit of love, and the parents' work is bringing the child to maturity. Not only the child: we become aware that the slender and youthful pair are themselves maturing as they unite in this activity. The child seems to like its lesson, but that is not the point. Love must be able to say no as well as yes, and even to seem unloving if, in the end, that is for the other's betterment.

The First Steps (after Millet), 1890, Vincent van Gogh
28¹/₂ x 36 in (72 x 91 cm), oil on canvas
Metropolitan Museum of Art, New York

CHASING THE BUTTERFLY

PARENTAL LOVE is potentially its purest form, and may be the most painful. Gainsborough, whose marriage was unhappy, adored his two daughters, whom he called Molly and the Captain. Their mother's flawed psyche was inherited by both girls, and their father agonized over them all his life. Neither was to know happiness, and his many pictures of them show a sad foreknowledge of this. To give those we love their independence, to accept that we cannot make their choices for them, that they cannot live by our hard-earned experience: this is part of love. We have to allow those dear to us to chase the butterfly, however convinced we are that it is uncatchable. We can never give the butterfly of happiness to another: each must catch it alone. For some, it will be ever elusive, and love must work within that painful understanding.

Chasing the Butterfly, c.1755-6, Thomas Gainsborough
44³/₄ x 41¹/₄ in (114 x 105 cm), oil on canvas
National Gallery, London

THE GAZE OF LOVE

IF LOVE EXISTS UNDER ALL CIRCUMSTANCES, then so do the objects of love. There is always beauty to be found. It may not be for our possessing, but learning detachment is part of respect. The world is there

despite us yet, and if we are not greedy, it is there *for* us. Zurbarán sets four vessels in a row; he lets the sun shine on them. He gazes in awe at their simple elegance, captivated by the sheer actuality of their shapes, by the shadows they cast and the play of light on their coloring. He makes no statement; he simply delights, and gives thanks. Because of his reverence, Zurbarán allows the magic that is visible to him to become apparent to our eyes too.

Love communicates.

Still Life, 1635
Francisco de Zurbarán
18 x 33 in (46 x 84 cm)
oil on canvas
Museo del Prado, Madrid, Spain

PARTING

ALL LOVE, whether of child, parent, partner, friend, even of place, possession, or animal, holds the potential for suffering, because of death. We cannot possess or hold fast anything or anyone: it is all gift. Life contains inevitable partings and inescapable pain. The loveless are protected against this suffering: the zombie feels nothing. We are alive in proportion to our response to love, and our pain at parting is in proportion to the extent of that love. Altdorfer's leave-taking is a wonderfully unsentimental depiction of what it means to say good-bye. He glorifies none of his characters: Mary has enormous feet, thrust almost violently upon the viewer's attention. Christ and his disciples are ready to move out into a world of possibilities; his mother and her companion women must stay, imprisoned in the decay of their old environment. For them, the sun is setting: Christ is aware of it, compassionate yet still resolute. It is his vocation to go, and though his mother grieves, so it has to be. The deeper the love, the deeper its pain.

Christ Taking Leave of His Mother, c.1520, Albrecht Altdorfer
54 x 43¹/₂ in (141 x 111 cm), oil on wood panel
National Gallery, London

REGRET

NONE OF US can claim a perfect record in love. We all fail and betray, even inadvertently. This is perhaps the worst pain of love, failure for which we feel culpable. The Magdalen, having come to love Christ after a life of selfishness, grieved forever after. Donatello shows her in old age, his fragile wooden carving furrowed with the marks of her long penance. She is literally abraded to the bone by sadness for what might have been, and yet her beauty is still luminous with hope for what is still to come. This is a vision of what all love knows: repentance for inadequacy.

The Magdalen, 1453-55, Donatello
73 in (185 cm), gilt and painted wood
Museo dell'Opera del Duomo, Florence

CONDITIONAL LOVE

PERHAPS THE MOST enduring failure in love is that of not revealing one's true self. The temptation to seem better than one is, not to risk the rejection truth might bring, is a perpetual one. We need great faith in the reality of love to dare to present ourselves in naked trust to the person we love. This brightly attired young man shows us the beguiling charm of his gesture. But he carries a bird that is caged: if we conceal our true selves before love, then we keep the bird safe only in confinement. Open the cage, and the bird can truly live.

Chelsea porcelain, 1759
7 in (18.5 cm), porcelain
Private collection

ABSOLUTE TRUST

THERE CAN BE NO LOVE without trust, yet it must be an intelligent trust. Love is not blind, despite the saying, and we cannot truly give our hearts to the unknown. The story of Abraham and his only son Isaac has always been a daunting one. Abraham believed that God was calling him to sacrifice his son, and he was saved from this hideous action only at the last minute. I have a personal reading of this story: to me the only one that makes sense. It is that God would never ask us to do something that is evil, and Abraham must have known this. So what we have is two gigantic acts of trust, each based upon knowledge of the other person, and of God. Abraham could only have gone ahead in the absolute belief that the horror would never happen. Isaac, for his

Sacrifice of Abraham, 1994, Albert Herbert
7³/₄ x 8 in (20 x 20.5 cm), oil on zinc
Private collection

part, submitted to being bound and laid on the altar, believing against all appearances that his father would not harm him. If Abraham had not known God, if Isaac had not known his father, such trust would have been madness. Love insists that we make a true judgment and then cleave to it, whatever the appearances.

OBSESSION

LOVE CAN BE MISDIRECTED. If we choose, we can fix our hearts unavailingly. Narcissus fell in love with himself. He pined to death, longing for a response that of its nature could not come: it was his own reflection he was courting. Echo fell in love with him, despite the evidence that he had no eyes for anyone but himself. She faded to a voice on the breeze, and he to a flower. As Poussin shows it, she is already dematerializing, unable or unwilling to accept reality. Beautiful Narcissus is visibly losing strength as he yearns for the self he sees in the waters. Poussin makes no judgment, but he reveals both as passive. True love (Cupid with his torch) lingers regretfully in the background.

Love in itself is alive and active.

Echo and Narcissus, c.1628–30, Nicolas Poussin
29 x 39¹/₂ in (74 x 100 cm), oil on canvas
Musée du Louvre, Paris

BEYOND THE CAVE

ARTHUR BOYD TAKES the myth of Narcissus and sets it in the contemporary Australian landscape. Yet it could be an archetypal landscape, a nowhere place of sand and sea and distant scrub. Narcissus is enclosed in the dragon cave of his own mind. Boyd suggests another reading of the myth, the passion for self-knowledge. Narcissus seems to be seeking not so much his self, in an egoistic sense, as insight *into* self, something wholly different and worthy of dedication. Yet it is outside the confines of his cave that the orange tree blooms: love requires selflessness. Narcissus squats as he paws the pool, stiff with anxious desire. He even seems to lose his humanness, a reflected tail bestializing him. Whatever the motive, love must range abroad — not be confined to the self. The whole world is there for loving, but we must venture outside ourselves to discover it.

Cave, Narcissus, and Orange Tree, 1976, Arthur Boyd
60 x 48 in (152 x 122 cm), oil on board
Savill Galleries, Sydney, Australia

THE FORTRESS

HOWEVER HAZARDOUS the development of love may be, love itself is a certain blessing. To love means to put someone or something before oneself, to rise above the pettiness of the ego, and in that we can never go amiss. Ken Kiff shows a very bleak world indeed. The sky is the darkest black, and even the moon or sun is a clouded ball. In its occluded

illumination we can make out a shriveled tree, as stark as seaweed, and beside it a pale rock. In this arid world, a flower lifts up its leaves in a gesture of rejoicing. Its petals glow with sweet vitality: whatever else is dead here, this small bloom is joyfully and brightly alive. Love, in fact, cannot be extinguished. No black sky or dying trees can affect its inner radiance.

*Flower and
Black Sky
1987–88
Ken Kiff
7 x 17¼ in
(18 x 44 cm)
water-color
Marlborough
Fine Art Ltd,
London*

AGELESS LOVE

IF LOVE CANNOT be killed, neither can it be diminished. Whatever the changes in the loved one, true love stays firm. It will deepen, but not lessen. Bonnard began to live with Marthe, later his wife, when both were young. As they aged, Marthe became progressively neurotic, spending hours each day in the bathtub. He painted her there, year after year, never seeing her as aging or being in any way different from the slender girl of his first affections. It is not Marthe herself he paints, wrinkled and exasperating, but her spirit, the perpetual beauty of what she essentially is to him, radiant in the clear water, rainbowed in the light. This is how it felt to love Marthe, how all love that is genuine feels. There is no art without love.

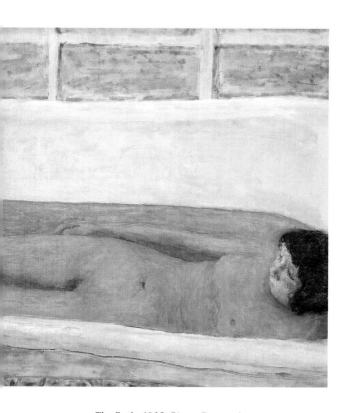

The Bath, 1925, Pierre Bonnard
33³/₄ x 47¹/₂ in (86 x 120.5 cm), oil on canvas
Tate Gallery, London

FORGETTING SELF

IT IS EXTREMELY difficult to love unselfishly. We aspire to it, because the moment we subordinate the other's needs to our own, the moment we use them, we have, for that moment, ceased to love. Being selfish, a user, and regretting it, overcoming it, starting again; this is one of life's patterns. Death of a beloved can be an acid test; we are being abandoned, even if unintentionally. Utter concentration on the other in such a time of crisis is very rare. That is what makes Monet's picture so extraordinary. Camille was his wife. Her early death left Monet not only bereft of her companionship but with small children now fully dependent on him. Obviously, Monet is to some extent escaping the pain by externalizing it, but it is, nonetheless, a remarkable act of egoless activity. He forgets himself in catching the least glimmer of light on his wife's face. In itself, this self-forgetfulness is the essence of true commitment.

Camille on Her Deathbed, 1879, Claude Monet
35 1/2 x 26 3/4 in (90 x 68 cm), oil on canvas
Musée d'Orsay, Paris

PERFECT LOVE

ERFECT LOVE MAKES NO DEMANDS and seeks nothing for itself. This extraordinary and beautiful carving of Christ and St. John shows us that there is no such thing as right and wrong love, since, for it to be love at all, the other's happiness comes first.

St. John Resting on the Bosom of Christ, early 14th century
Master Heinrich of Constance
55 1/2 in (141 cm), wood
Mayer Van den Bergh Museum, Antwerp

SYMBOL OF LOVE

I N THE END, love is to be practiced rather than written out. Howard Hodgkin's *Fruit* does not attempt to paint a real fruit, but rather to recall and to celebrate the thing that has given such delight. It is a tiny picture, with several layerings of rich red border, but the remembered fruit escapes its confines, overwhelming the viewer with its richness and glory. He is painting a memory of intensity, choosing it as his theme, forgetting himself in appreciation of it. This is the perfect symbol of what it is to love.

Fruit, 1988-89, Howard Hodgkin
13 x 16 in (32.5 x 40.5 cm), oil on wood
Private collection

INDEX

PICTURE CREDITS

Every effort has been made to trace the copyright holders and we apologise in advance for any unintentional omissions. We would be pleased to insert the appropriate acknowledgement in any subsequent edition of this publication.

Endpapers Reproduced by courtesy of the Trustees of the National Gallery, London
p5 Reproduced by courtesy of the Trustees of the National Gallery, London
p7 Musée d'Orsay, Paris
p9 Österreichische Galerie, Vienna/Artothek
p11 Rijksmuseum, Amsterdam
pp12-13 Private Collection
pp14-15 Reproduced by courtesy of the Trustees of the National Gallery, London
p17 Musée d'Orsay, Paris
pp18-19 The Metropolitan Museum of Art, Gift of George N. and Helen M. Richard, 1964. (64.165.2) Photograph by Malcolm Varon ©1985 By The Metropolitan Museum of Ar
pp20-21 Reproduced by courtesy of the Trustees of the National Gallery, London
pp22-23 ©Museo del Prado, Madrid. All rights reserved
p25 Reproduced by courtesy of the Trustees of the National Gallery, London
pp26 Museo dell'Opera del Duomo, Florence
p27 Private Collection
p29 Private Collection, Courtesy England & Co. Gallery, London
pp30-31 Musée du Louvre, Paris
p33 Courtesy Savill Galleries, Sydney

pp34-35 Courtesy of Marlborough Fine Art Ltd
pp36-37 The Tate Gallery, London/ ©ADAGP/ SPADEM, Paris and DACS, London 1995
p39 Musée d'Orsay, Paris
p41 Museum Mayer van den Bergh, Antwerpen
pp42-43 Collection Mary Tyler Moore and Dr. S. Robert Levine, courtesy Anthony d'Offay Gallery

Photography for Dorling Kindersley
p26 Alison Harris;
p39 Susannah Price;
pp7, 17, 30-31 Philippe Sebert

JACKET PICTURE CREDITS

Fra Angelico
Christ Glorified in the Court of Heaven (detail)

Ascribed to Geertgen
The Nativity at Night (detail)

Style of Orcagna
Small Altarpiece: The Crucifixion (detail)

Reproduced by courtesy of the Trustees of the National Gallery, London